sport snaps
monte dutton

Jeff Gordon

the racer

To Zona N. Dutton, my grandmother,
a guiding influence on my life and,
coincidentally, quite a fan of Jeff Gordon's.

M.D.

PHOTO CREDITS:

Allsport
Front Cover [D. Taylor], 1 [C. Jones], 6 [D. Taylor],
7 [J. Squire], 8 [D. Taylor], 10 [D. Taylor],
11 [J. Squire], 12 [J. Ferrey], 15 [D. Taylor],
16 [D. Taylor], 18 [D. Taylor], 24 [J. Ferrey],
26 [D. Taylor], 29 [J. Squire], 30 [D. Taylor],
32 [J. Ferrey], 33 [J. Ferrey], 35 [R. Laberge],
36 [C. Jones], 37 [S. Swope], 38 [J. Ferrey],
39 [D. Taylor], 42 [D. Taylor], 45 [D. Taylor],
46 [D. Taylor].

AP/World Wide Photos
3, 14, 22, 25, 34, 44, 47, 48, 50, 51, 52, 53, 54,
55 top, 55 bottom.

BBS
56 [B. Westerholt].

UPI
20, 28, 40.

The Charlotte Observer
4 [C. Record], 5 [C. Record].

Monte Dutton's photo courtesy of Tom Whitmore.

Printed by Pinnacle Press, Inc.
in the United States of America.

Designed by Werremeyer | Floresca.

LIBRARY OF CONGRESS
CATALOG CARD NUMBER 00-104934

table of contents

the day

JEFF GORDON WILL NEVER FORGET

The Kid wasn't supposed to win this way. He was supposed to ram his Chevy hard into some fourth turn, risking life and limb, and somehow come out of the smoke and fire in first place.

Instead, Jeff Gordon captured his first Winston Cup victory, in the Coca-Cola 600 at what was then known as Charlotte Motor Speedway, by calmly pulling off a strategic move that would have made all his wily predecessors – Richard Petty, David Pearson, et al. – proud.

The skinny youth, far less imposing than the rainbow-bright Chevy he manhandled, wept in victory lane.

"If there's a feeling any higher than this, I don't know it," he stammered, self-conscious and obviously worried about saying the wrong thing.

Then the governor of North Carolina, Jim Hunt, walked up to bask in the reflection of Gordon's glow.

"Thank you, Governor, this is a memory I'm never going to forget," said Gordon, shredding his caution. "This is the highlight of my life."

"How old are you, son? Twenty-two?" asked His Honor.

"Yeah," said Gordon, "and life is just as great as it could ever be."

On May 29, 1994, on a lovely evening under the Charlotte lights, the dominance of four drivers – Dale Earnhardt, Rusty Wallace, Ernie Irvan and Mark Martin – suddenly seemed tenuous. Their hold on the hearts of the fans suddenly had new competition. Gordon had already been hailed as the sport's next superstar.

By winning the sport's longest race on the track that, on race days, becomes its unofficial capital, Gordon had arrived.

JEFF GORDON profile

24

BORN:

AUGUST 4, 1971,
VALLEJO, CALIFORNIA.

FAMILY:

WIFE, BROOKE.

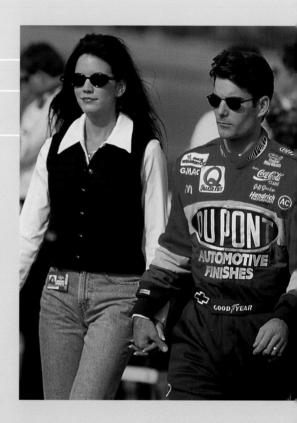

IS THERE ANY PLACE WHERE YOU
AND BROOKE 'GET AWAY FROM IT ALL'?
"I don't know why, but people don't seem
to make such a fuss when Brooke and I
go out to a movie. Usually, when we visit
a theater, we can go and be treated like
anybody else. I don't know if it's because
race fans don't go to movies that much,
or whether it's because people recognize
the need for privacy when you're trying to
watch a movie, but we've never had any
trouble being mobbed by fans at the
movies. Usually, we arrive at a Cineplex,
stand in line for tickets just like everybody
else, go in, buy some popcorn or
whatever, and enjoy the show."

Jeff Gordon is vitally interested in two charities, The Bone Marrow Foundation and the Make-A-Wish Foundation.

Gordon first became acquainted with the Bone Marrow Foundation when the son of long-time crew chief Ray Evernham contracted leukemia. Later the owner of Gordon's No. 24 DuPont Chevrolet, Rick Hendrick, also was diagnosed with the dreaded disease. Both required bone marrow transplants, and both have been fortunate enough to have the disease go into remission.

The three-time Winston Cup champion spends considerable time participating in Make-A-Wish Foundation activities. It is not unusual to see Gordon spending time at the track with youngsters referred to him by the Make-A-Wish Foundation.

Gordon is in the process of forming his own foundation to serve as a clearinghouse for his charitable activities.

WHAT KIND OF MOVIES DO YOU LIKE?
"I really like the action and adventure films. If you'd ask me my favorite movie, I'd have to think about it, but probably I'd answer something like 'Crimson Tide.' Brooke is more a fan of romantic comedies. She really likes 'Sleepless in Seattle' and other films like that. I guess you could say that our movie tastes have grown closer together. I've developed a greater appreciation for her favorite movies, and she has developed a taste for action/adventure films like 'Face/Off' and 'Speed.' One movie that kind of combines both types is 'Titanic.' Both of us were just blown away by that movie. You couldn't ask for more of an adventure in terms of special effects, but at the same time, it's a classic love story. The love affair that develops between Leonardo DiCaprio and Kate Winslet is really cool. Plus, it has a sad ending that is kind of uplifting and inspirational in its own way. We both love that movie."

JEFF GORDON, IT IS SAID, WAS A SOLITARY KID, ADVENTUROUS BUT, AT THE SAME TIME, SOMEWHAT THE LONER. RATHER THAN PLAY "COPS AND ROBBERS" WITH A BAND OF NEIGHBORHOOD KIDS, LITTLE JEFF WOULD FACE DOWN HIS IMAGINARY NEMESES ALONE. USUALLY THEY WERE INANIMATE OBJECTS: LONG, STEEP BANKS TO BE CONQUERED WITH HIS BICYCLE, OR MAKESHIFT JUMPS.

8th

NASCAR | ranked eighth in all-time victories

He was destined to compete as an individual, alone in the cockpit of his trusty race car.

The only reason he ever got into a race car was the fact that his mother, Carol, fretted over the number of times he tumbled off his bicycle, or his skateboard, or his roller skates.

"I think Jeff Gordon is the best driver of all time."

FELIX SABATES, RIVAL CAR OWNER

In his stepfather, John Bickford, Jeff found a willing conspirator. In Jeff, Bickford saw the glimmer of talent. Bickford was the type of man who would go to the ends of the earth to promote something or someone he believed in. In his stepson's case, that ended up being Indiana.

It all started with quarter midgets. They were safer than bicycle races, Bickford and the boy argued to Carol. They even had safety equipment. Jeff would wear a helmet, even a uniform. She went along with the plans cautiously, like most moms who consider all men to be children to one extent or another. The first track was a trail cut through a field of weeds. Jeff was 5 years old when he began racing quarter midgets. He never even remembered his first feature event until years later, when Bickford produced an audiotape he had made at the time.

At age 7, Jeff won 36 quarter-midget main events and ran the fastest lap in every event he entered. Quick study, that kid.

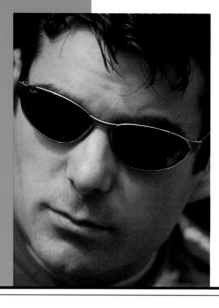

Bickford was Jeff's Svengali, or perhaps his Bela Karolyi. He paid diligent attention to the minutest of details. The brilliant kid had a meticulous father.

By 1981, Jeff was racing go-karts, too. In one year, he won 25 go-kart races and a national championship in quarter midgets. At 13, he was too accomplished to continue in karts and quarter midgets and too young to drive anything bigger according to the laws of the State of California. No problem, said Bickford, who promptly moved the family to Indiana so that the boy could race sprints and midgets. By 16, Jeff had earned a full competition license from the United States Auto Club.

Tips for Young Fans:
VISIT YOUR LOCAL SHORT TRACKS

DON'T JUST DEPEND ON THE SUPERSPEEDWAYS TO TEACH YOU ALL YOU NEED TO KNOW ABOUT NASCAR. TO UNDERSTAND THE GRASSROOTS ESSENCE OF STOCK CAR RACING, MAKE A VISIT TO YOUR LOCAL SHORT TRACK. A TYPICAL SHORT-TRACK PROGRAM FEATURES COMPETITION IN SEVERAL CLASSES, AND THE SHORTER LENGTH OF THE RACES WILL HOLD YOUR INTEREST. IF YOU FIRST GAIN AN UNDERSTANDING OF THE SPORT FROM THIS PERSPECTIVE, IT WILL BE MUCH EASIER FOR YOU TO APPRECIATE THE NUANCES OF THE 400- AND 500-MILERS.

"He won the night-before-the-500 midget race at 17. That's, like, not done."

BOB EAST, FOR WHOM GORDON DROVE OPEN-WHEEL CARS

Were there times when the boy wonder chafed at the constant pressure under which he was operating? Sure. In the summer of 1983, Bickford sensed the burnout, so he abruptly sent Jeff to water-skiing school. Racing stopped cold. They took several breaks, just to let the kid see how much he missed the competition. "Each time," said Bickford, "Jeff came back 'stimulated and better focused.'"

At every level, success came naturally. Jeff's career became the object of a national cult following, thanks to the cable-television exposure of the "Thunder" shows on ESPN. Bickford advised Jeff to forget about winning a national championship in the sprints and midgets and instead run a schedule based on television exposure. Other men, most notably the great midget and sprint-car designer Bob East, prepared the cars, but it was Bickford who taught his stepson the trappings of success.

"I used to tell Jeff, 'If you waddle into the kitchen like a duck, if you conduct yourself like a duck, eventually somebody will think you're a duck. If you act like a race-car driver, maybe somebody will actually think you're a race-car driver,'" Bickford recalled early in 1998.

Tips for Young Fans:
THERE'S NO SUBSTITUTE
FOR BEING AT A TRACK,
SEEING THE RACE

TELEVISION OFFERS EXCELLENT COVERAGE OF NASCAR RACING, BUT THERE IS NO SUBSTITUTE FOR BEING THERE. FOR SOME REASON, THE INCREDIBLE SPECTACLE OF CARS RUNNING BUMPER-TO-BUMPER DOES NOT FULLY TRANSLATE TO THE SMALL SCREEN, PARTICULARLY THE ACTION AT A SHORT TRACK LIKE THE ONE IN MARTINSVILLE, VA. TRY TO GET TO THE TRACK SEVERAL TIMES A YEAR. IT WILL MAKE YOU MORE PERCEPTIVE THE NEXT TIME YOU WATCH A RACE ON TV.

#2

"Last year [1998] Jeff didn't win all the races, just 13.

It's not like he doesn't have anything left to achieve."

JOHN BICKFORD, GORDON'S STEPFATHER

"I won a lot when I was very young," Gordon said. "My parents kept me humble then, and I think I'm still humble today. The biggest part of my success is the race team. They just go out there every week and do their job, and it's the same thing for me."

Did the kingmaker envision that his prize pupil
would become the most celebrated figure in
American motorsports?

"Heck, no," Bickford said. "How can a parent imagine that? Maybe in our wildest
dreams, yes, but who could have known that, at 27, my kid would have his own
jet, a motor coach, millions of dollars in yearly earnings. I didn't see that coming.
I just had a kid with talent, and I wanted him to see it through."

IN 1988, JOHN BICKFORD ACTUALLY PLACED A CALL TO DALE EARNHARDT, THE MOST FAMOUS FIGURE IN NASCAR, TO ASK FOR ADVICE IN DIRECTING THE CAREER OF HIS STEPSON. BICKFORD COULD NOT REACH EARNHARDT DIRECTLY, BUT THE SEVEN-TIME WINSTON CUP CHAMPION (AT THAT TIME HE HAD WON ONLY THREE) SENT WORD BACK. EVEN EARNHARDT HAD HEARD OF THE KID WHO WAS TEARING UP THE OPEN-WHEEL TRACKS OF THE MIDWEST.

NASCAR | best career winning percentage: .2197

The message sent back by Earnhardt was: "Tell him
to get off the dirt and learn how to save tires."

Gordon, at the time, seemed destined for Indianapolis,
not Daytona. In the late 1980s, he was trying to get into
other open-wheel series – the American Racing Series,
or perhaps Toyota Atlantic. The experience was frustrating:
Gordon's career had reached a level that was beyond
Bickford's ability to make deals on his behalf.

Examining all options, Gordon traveled to Rockingham, N.C.,
and the Buck Baker Driving School, where he sampled stock
cars. At lunch, he telephoned his stepfather.

"Sell everything," Gordon said. "We're going stock car racing."

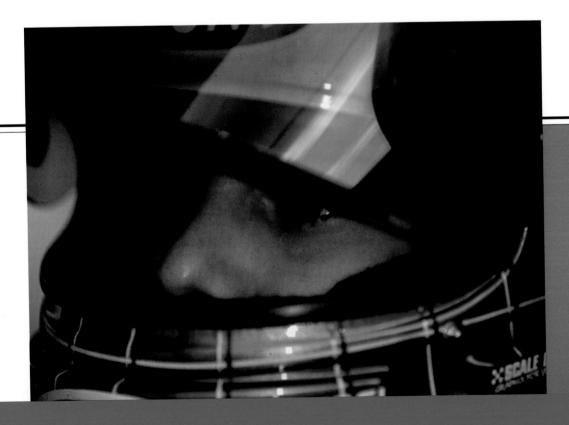

At that moment, what was about to happen to stock car racing was comparable in relative impact to the introduction of nuclear weapons into World War II. The NASCAR world would never be the same again.

During 1990, Gordon's first year in stock cars, he competed in only a handful of events, but he began working closely with Ray Evernham, a former New Jersey modified driver who had abruptly decided to move south to pursue a career as a mechanic. In a test that summer at the track then known as Charlotte Motor Speedway, Gordon experienced difficulty getting his stock car properly through the 1.5-mile track's third turn. A more experienced driver was even brought in to assist Gordon, but it was Evernham who tirelessly pushed the talented phenom until, finally, Gordon found "the line."

"I know him, and I know him real well. He's a real good person."

RAY EVERNHAM, FORMER GORDON CREW CHIEF

That night Gordon called his stepfather. "You're gonna like Ray Evernham," he told Bickford. "He never gives up. He's just like you."

Ford Motor Company helped Gordon find a ride with a team in the Busch Series, NASCAR's version of the Triple-A minor leagues. Arkansas businessman Bill Davis, who had run a limited schedule with Winston Cup regular Mark Martin, hired Gordon to drive his Thunderbird in 1991. Evernham continued as Gordon's crew chief.

Late in 1990, Gordon qualified second for a race, but his finishes were subpar. Davis decided to hire him anyway. In 1991, Gordon had five top-five finishes and ten top 10s. The following year Gordon won three races, all on "superspeedways" (tracks of one mile or larger), and set a Busch Grand National record of 11 poles.

The plan, in 1993, was for Gordon to move into Winston Cup with Davis. Enter Rick Hendrick.

The Charlotte car dealer was already owner of one of NASCAR's premier teams. Luring Gordon to his team, and from Ford to Chevrolet, became Hendrick's master stroke. Davis had been unable to nail down a sponsor, and Gordon eventually signed a three-year contract to drive for Hendrick, with sponsorship from DuPont Automotive Finishes. Evernham moved with Gordon.

Tips for Young Fans:
READ LOCAL NEWSPAPERS
TO LEARN WHEN NASCAR
COMES TO YOUR AREA

ONE OF THE PRIMARY REASONS WHY RACE-CAR DRIVERS ARE SO ATTENTIVE TO THE NEEDS OF THEIR FANS IS THE COMMITMENT REQUIRED OF THE DRIVERS BY THEIR SPONSORS. THE COMMERCIAL NATURE OF THE SPORT REQUIRES THAT DRIVERS LEARN QUICKLY THAT THEY HAVE OBLIGATIONS TO THE GENERAL PUBLIC. KEEP AN EYE ON LOCAL NEWSPAPERS WHEN NASCAR COMES TO YOUR AREA. YOU'LL BE SURPRISED AT HOW MANY DRIVERS MAKE APPEARANCES AT SHOPPING MALLS, RESTAURANTS AND OTHER LOCAL BUSINESSES.

#3

"The first time I ever saw Jeff was in a Busch car," said Hendrick, "and I was immediately impressed by how he could drive so fast and out of control. He was the only person I had ever seen whose driving style reminded me of [the late] Tim Richmond. That's why I signed him."

"In the history of motorsports, I've never seen a talent quite like him."

RICK HENDRICK, CAR OWNER

At the time, Gordon was harshly criticized for leaving both Davis and Ford, both of whom had been his benefactors. The split was bitter.

"Time has healed those wounds," said Davis, who moved up to Winston Cup anyway with Bobby Labonte, who competed against Gordon and Kenny Wallace in the Winston Cup rookie-of-the-year race. "I guess I look back now and realize Jeff did what, at the time, he had to do. At that time, I could no longer offer him what Rick Hendrick could."

Jeff Gordon's first year in the Winston Cup Series — the actual debut had occurred in the 1992 season finale — was remarkable by contemporary standards, but noteworthy for his sense of the dramatic rather than for week-to-week consistency.

$9,306,584

NASCAR RECORD | money won, single season: $9,306,584

For instance, prior to his very first Daytona 500, Gordon
drove his rainbow-colored Chevrolet to victory in one of
the two 125-mile qualifying races held annually to help
determine the 500's starting lineup. He also won a pole
and twice finished second, with five other top-five finishes
and 11 finishes in the top 10. He finished 14th in the
season point standings.

Gordon also carried on a secret, season-long romance
with Miss Winston, Brooke Sealy, whom he met in February
1993 after winning the Daytona qualifier. Since the tobacco
company forbade its beauty queens from dating drivers,
Jeff and Brooke carefully kept the developing romance
under wraps until her tenure as beauty queen was
completed. They married shortly afterward.

"That's the first thing I saw in Jeff that made me love him," said the new Mrs. Gordon. "When we first started seeing each other, at UNCC (the University of North Carolina at Charlotte, where she was a student), he didn't act any different from everybody else. He didn't act like somebody famous, even though he was."

Gordon's marriage changed him in many ways. Brooke Gordon directed her husband toward the finer things in life. He became more discerning about his appearance, gave up the "jeans and T-shirts" wardrobe of his short-track days and learned that life did not begin and end at the gates of racetracks.

Soon, Gordon was proving himself to be as adept as a corporate spokesman as he was as a race-car driver maneuvering 3,400-pound stock cars on NASCAR's high banks. With his boyish good looks and colorful driving style, he became the symbol of an entire generation of younger fans and NASCAR's emergence into the mainstream of the American sports scene.

"When I raced Jeff in the Busch Series, he was wearing Reebok tennis shoes, jeans, sweatshirts, T-shirts, but Jeff today is still a great person," said fellow driver Kenny Wallace. "The only thing that has changed about Jeff, out of everything, is that he married a model, and she straightened him out. She got his old scraggly mustache shaved off.

"Brooke Gordon is a great lady who has shown Jeff the world.... It is truly Brooke who has changed Jeff, and that is not at all a bad thing. But when it's just me and Jeff, one on one, he's still the same 'Jeff Gord' from 1991."

Another effect Brooke had was that she brought her husband closer to God.

"I had never known about God," Jeff said. "I mean, my whole life had been wrapped up in my career, and while I had always believed there was a God, it was not something I had pondered. Brooke helped me understand the meaning of life."

"Jeff and I came from different backgrounds," added Brooke. "Going to church had always been a part of my life, but Jeff had never had a chance to experience what was a normal part of my life and a normal part of most people's lives."

The 1994 season was another stepping stone for the soon-to-be champion, who once again demonstrated his flair for the dramatic. Gordon's two official victories occurred in big-ticket events, the Coca-Cola 600, NASCAR's longest event, and the Brickyard 400, NASCAR's first visit to world-renowned Indianapolis Motor Speedway. He improved to eighth in the season standings.

The storm was building. In 1995, Gordon finally hit the stock car establishment with the full force of his talent.

NASCAR | all-time victories, modern era: sixth

" I don't necessarily hate him.
I get tired of
seeing him win
all the time."

BOBBY HAMILTON, FELLOW DRIVER

Over the next four years, Gordon won three championships and missed the other by a scant 37 points. He won 40 races, including a Daytona 500 in 1997 and a second Brickyard in 1998. He became the first driver in stock car racing's modern era to win 10 or more races three years in a row (1996-98) and tied Richard Petty's record (also for the 1972-present modern era) for victories in a season with 13 in '98. He became the first driver to win four consecutive Southern 500s – Darlington Raceway had been holding the event since 1950 – and the only driver in history to win five consecutive races on road courses.

Gordon revolutionized the sport, as much as any man –
Richard Petty, Dale Earnhardt – who had come before him.

At one point, Gordon won 40 times in a span of 127 races, above
31 percent. In the most productive five-year stretch of Petty's
35-year (1958-92) career, the man known to his fans as "The King"
won 92 times in 233 events, which, to be fair, was a higher
percentage (.395) than Gordon's. In Petty's heyday, however,
there were many more races and many less competitive cars.
Most experts would concede that, given the growth of the sport,
Gordon's .315 percentage during his most prolific period to date
was, at the very least, comparable to Petty's golden era.

"You take advantage of everything you get and savor the moment," Gordon said quietly, "because you never know if you're going to get another one. It's been an incredible four-year run for us. Three championships and one second, and my teammate [Terry Labonte] won the other one. Those odds are all against you, and somehow, they've been working in my favor the last three or four years. I don't know what to say.

"If I have years like I had this year, I'll race as long as I possibly can," he said at the end of 1998. "The likelihood of that happening for 20 years, I don't see it. I don't put an age or number on it. I think it really has to do with being competitive and being physically in good enough shape to go out there and do it. I've worked hard on my schedule away from the race track to make sure I don't get burned out. It's all the things away from the track that burn you out."

Gordon lives in a world in which successful people relish in throwing their success in other people's faces. Yet NASCAR does not have an imperial champion.

Almost everyone who watches Gordon from close by –
family, friends, other drivers, associates, journalists –
likes him. Somehow, those who look at him from a
distance seem to see something entirely different.
Gordon is not particularly gregarious. What modest
person is? He doesn't talk constantly, seldom slaps
anyone on the back when he greets him and goes out
of his way not to flaunt his mastery of the sport.

Tips for Young Fans:
SOMETIMES THE BEST
RACING IS NOT AT THE FRONT
OF THE TRACK

FORTY-THREE CARS START EACH WINSTON
CUP AND BUSCH GRAND NATIONAL RACE,
AND THE COMPETITION IS INTENSE
THROUGHOUT THE FIELD. KEEP AN EYE ON
THE SCOREBOARD, AND PAY ATTENTION TO
WHICH CARS ARE RACING FOR POSITION.
ALSO, WATCH THE VARIOUS LEADERS, AND
TRY TO PICK OUT WHICH DRIVERS SEEM
MOST ADEPT AT EFFICIENTLY WORKING
THEIR WAY THROUGH LAPPED TRAFFIC.
MORE OFTEN THAN NOT, THE DRIVER WHO
EVENTUALLY WINS IS THE ONE WITH THE
KNACK OF PASSING SLOWER CARS MOST
EFFICIENTLY.

#5

But he is a nice kid. A nice kid who, by the age
of 28, had won more races than anyone in history;
who, in 1998, earned more than $9 million in a
single year, easily the highest total in the history
of the sport; and who, without the advantage
of coming from a rich family or having any
appreciable education, blossomed into a
fabulously successful career and also became
a role model for the country's youth.

Gordon is also remarkably
unaffected by his unprecedented
success. How could this
possibly be?

"Several things," he said. "First, I've always been a race-car driver, and I'm still a race-car driver."

By that statement, he meant that, while he had business interests, he was not a businessman. While he was well-known, he was not, at least by outlook, a celebrity. The most important goal in Gordon's mind was winning the next race. He never loses sight of the task at hand.

"Brooke keeps me humble," he added. "We like to go to the movies. We go out to eat. We try to live our lives like any other couple. That's what keeps me humble. I don't see any reason why it [his fame] should go to my head. I'm living a dream life. Why risk it by throwing it in other people's faces?"

Off the track, Gordon is as predictable as the daily eastern rise of the sun. He shines more brightly than anyone in the NASCAR cosmos, and he does it every day.

"Gordon is tough. He's a great competitor. He may not look tough, and he may sound like a polite kid, but, believe me, on a race track, he's as tough as they come."

DALE EARNHARDT, SEVEN-TIME WINSTON CUP CHAMPION

In his public persona, Gordon does the right thing in the context of what a mother would want. He is polite, politically correct and well-mannered. When Gordon arrives in a public place away from the track, he has invariably combed his hair, and replaced his driving suit with a shirt and slacks that look like they just had the labels and pins removed. He handles his responsibilities with polish and aplomb.

"This is a big sport now," said Gordon. "There's a lot of money involved, a lot of sponsors with commitment to the drivers and crew chiefs. That keeps you busy, but you've got to learn how to say no. You've got to learn how to make sure you're fulfilling your commitments, but most of all, you've got to fulfill your commitment to the race team and to what is really making this all go around for you, which is performing in the car."

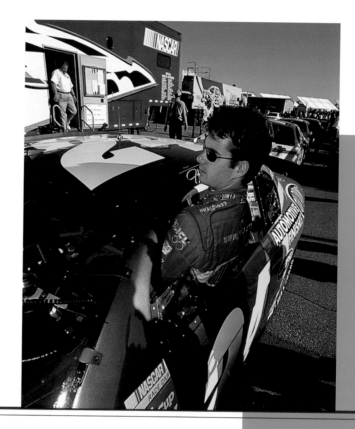

On the track, perhaps it is instructive to consult the only two seven-time champions in NASCAR history: Dale Earnhardt, still a worthy rival, and Richard Petty.

"He has that competitive nature, and I think, like most champion racers, you can see it in everything he does," said Earnhardt of Gordon. "I don't care whether it's racing or computer games or whatever he does, he's competitive and that's why he's a winner. He goes that extra mile. He works hard."

Yet somehow, Gordon, despite his legion of predominantly young fans, has never been as beloved as Petty, the only driver ever to attain comparable success at a comparable age.

"I was lucky," Petty said. "I think one of the things you've got to look at with my career is, when I was winning a lot of my races and forming my reputation, most of the fans were either General Motors fans or Ford fans, and I was driving a Plymouth. A lot of 'em didn't want nobody driving a Ford to win, and a lot of 'em were dead-set against anybody in a Chevrolet winning, but when I won, they didn't mind as much."

"Most of the people who don't like Gordon are people who don't know him," added Earnhardt. "He's a good guy, and he's someone who hasn't let all that success, and money and whatever, go to his head. If the fans give him a hard time, well, that's just something you've got to expect. If you're a Dale Earnhardt fan, or a Dale Jarrett fan or a Mark Martin fan or whoever, you're not going to be happy when Jeff Gordon wins the race. I really believe he understands that, so a lot more is made out of it by others than I think is really made out of it by him.

"Gordon's got his fans, and there's a lot of them. I went through the same thing. Darrell [Waltrip] went through the same thing. It's not like a football game, where one group is pulling for one team and the other group is pulling for the other. There are 43 cars on the race track, and with all his success, he's kind of become the threat to the fans of all 42 of the others. In that kind of a situation, you're going to get booed, and the fans have that right. They paid their way in, and being willing to do that is what keeps the rest of us in business."

Madison Avenue obviously considers Gordon to be the perfect stock car racer. In the grandstands, considerable evidence exists to suggest that many fans find him TOO perfect. From a distance, Gordon seems, well, distant to some of them. This world-renowned athlete must privately be frustrated that he does everything right, yet his detractors find something wrong even with that.

"Back when we were racing, David Pearson had us all beat 'between the ears,' and I never thought I'd see a racer smarter than Pearson. Jeff Gordon is smarter than Pearson, though.
He's the smartest race driver who ever lived."
BOBBY ALLISON

"I don't worry about that," said Gordon. "I'm just thankful for the great fans I do have. I understand why it is that sometimes I get booed. Every driver has his fans, and maybe when I win several races, I guess I get to be the biggest threat, the guy that's gonna keep their guy from winning. I understand that, and I don't think they mean anything by it."

Gordon's entourage never has to fret about worrisome behavior. The deeply religious Gordon is on pace to become the greatest stock car racer ever, and sometimes it seems that almost no one who doesn't wear a suit to work is willing to give him any credit for it.

"Some say he's the best driver out there," noted another of Gordon's rivals, Mark Martin. "Everyone knows he's got a fast car. You put that combination together and you've got an awfully impressive force to deal with. That's the reality."

By 1999, and the age of 28, Jeff Gordon had already had a hall-of-fame career. If he had retired at the end of 1998, he would have ranked 14th in stock car racing history in victories, despite having competed for only six seasons. Only two men, Dale Earnhardt and Richard Petty, had won more championships. His career winning percentage, .222, would have been easily the best in NASCAR history.

17

GORDON | tracks on which he has won: 17

Of course, Gordon never considered retiring. In racing, where drivers in their 40s routinely win races and even championships, Gordon was still one of the younger stars.

Gordon's extraordinary level of success, particularly in 1996-98, was unprecedented and also probably impossible to sustain.

"Jeff has supreme confidence in himself.

He knows he has the potential to be the greatest driver ever."

JIMMY JOHNSON, FORMER HENDRICK MOTORSPORTS
GENERAL MANAGER

In the 1999 season, Gordon won more races, seven, than any other driver. He encored his 1997 victory in the Daytona 500, outdueling Dale Earnhardt. All that was lacking was consistency, and as a result, despite 18 top-five finishes, Gordon fell to sixth in the Winston Cup point standings, his worst finish since 1994.

The magical partnership between Gordon and crew chief, Ray Evernham, also unraveled. After a period of fruitless negotiations at Hendrick Motorsports, Evernham announced in late September that he would be leaving to head up Dodge's impending entry into the sport, effective in 2001.

Tips for Young Fans:
IF YOU ARE A YOUNG FAN, FIND
A YOUNG DRIVER TO FOLLOW

WITH A LITTLE LUCK, IDENTIFYING WITH
A YOUNG DRIVER WILL GIVE YOU YEARS
OF ENJOYMENT WATCHING THAT DRIVER IN
ACTION. MANY RACE FANS ESTABLISH
FAVORITE DRIVERS THROUGH CAR BRAND
LOYALTY. A FAN WHO DRIVES A CHEVROLET
OFTEN FINDS HIMSELF DRAWN TO A JEFF
GORDON OR A DALE EARNHARDT. ONE OF
THE SECRETS BEHIND THE FAMOUS LOYALTY
OF BILL ELLIOTT FANS IS THAT ELLIOTT HAS
SPENT PRACTICALLY HIS ENTIRE CAREER
DRIVING FORDS. IT WILL BE INTERESTING
TO SEE HOW ELLIOTT FANS RESPOND IN
2001, WHEN THEIR DRIVER MAKES THE
SWITCH TO A DODGE INTREPID.

Gordon found himself torn between two friendships: Evernham, a combination mechanic, coach and motivator; and Rick Hendrick, the owner who had weathered two years of painful treatment against the ravages of leukemia. When Gordon had to choose between the two, he chose the stability of Hendrick Motorsports.

"Things were getting stale," said Gordon, describing the last year he and Evernham were together. "Somehow the team had lost its luster."

No sooner had Evernham departed than Hendrick made a move to secure the future services of his star driver. In October, Gordon signed a lifetime contract with Hendrick Motorsports, one that gives him a share in ownership of one of the sport's most successful entities.

The Gordon flair for the dramatic made one more appearance late in the year, however. After his detractors predicted disaster upon Evernham's departure, Gordon promptly won the first two races, at Martinsville, Va., and Concord, N.C., with new crew chief Brian Whitesell in acting command of the team.

But even in the midst of celebration, Whitesell made a comment that proved fateful.

"I think I'm just breaking even," he said. "For every bit of the pressure I took off by winning, it added that much back on, simply because we've got to keep doing it."

In the final five races of the season, Gordon finished 12th, 11th, 10th, 10th and 39th. The difficulty finishing near the front was even more disquieting than worse finishes would have been had they been caused by crashes or mechanical failures. Tenth place was not a familiar position for Gordon.

Tips for Young Fans:
THOSE WHO SAY THE CARS ALL LOOK ALIKE ARE NOT REALLY WATCHING CLOSELY

TELLING A CHEVROLET MONTE CARLO FROM A FORD TAURUS, EVEN WITH THE MODIFICATIONS REQUIRED FOR RACING, IS EASIER THAN YOU THINK. FOR INSTANCE, THE REAR ROOFLINES ON THE TWO CARS ARE RADICALLY DIFFERENT. AND THE PONTIAC GRAND PRIX HAS A UNIQUE GRILLE THAT SEPARATES IT FROM THE MONTE CARLO AND TAURUS. MOST OF THE CARS NOW CARRY DECALS THAT SIMULATE THE DIFFERENT HEADLIGHT PLACEMENTS AND SHAPES.

#7

The team's manpower got a boost in the postseason when Robbie Loomis, previously at Petty Enterprises, became Gordon's crew chief. Whitesell was shuffled to the title team manager, taking on more administrative control.

The 2000 season also started poorly, and Gordon did not finish in the top five until the season's eighth race. What emerged from the slump was evidence of new maturity and patience in Gordon.

> **When I first noticed Gordon, I didn't think he was that good. Then I started watching him closely, and that's when I decided, he kind of reminds me of me."**
>
> DAVID PEARSON, WINNER OF 105 NASCAR RACES

"People's perception is that, if I'm not winning, I'm a miserable person," Gordon said. "If I based my life on what happens at the race track, compared to the success I've had in the past, then maybe I would be, but that's not what I make of my life on a day-to-day basis. My life means a lot more to me than that. I care about the things that are in it, and the people that are in it.

"These guys [his race team] are working their tails off. Some people have caught up to us and maybe moved ahead of us. We've got to get to where we are ahead of the game. We've got to figure out ways to make this car go faster. That's where we are right now."

But Gordon insisted that, in the total picture of his life with wife Brooke, he could separate success on the race track from happiness.

NASCAR RECORD | **consecutive superspeedway victories: 5**

five

"Away from the track, it doesn't matter if I finish 30th on Sunday," he said. "But I don't want people to think that success has made me care less about winning. That's not the case at all. There's nobody who gets more pumped up about wanting to go win a race, but I do try to keep an even-keel mind about it.

"I've been working out more, trying to get in better physical shape, trying to spend more time with the guys, and making sure that, mentally, we're all in this thing together. Racing is not what controls my life and the way I live it, and it doesn't determine whether, on Monday, I'm a happy person. I'm a happy person on Monday regardless of whether, on Sunday, I finished first or last."

Interestingly, Gordon pays no heed to superstition. "I've really gotten away from that," he said. "I used to be, maybe, a little superstitious. I think that my faith in God has taught me that there really are no superstitions. To me, I kind of know who's running the show, who's in charge. He's got His hands on it, so it doesn't matter what kind of superstitious things I do. That's not going to change His will.

"I've heard Max Helton (of Motor Racing Outreach) tell people that superstitions were OK, 'if you think it makes a difference, as long as you're not putting your faith in that. If it makes you feel good, then go ahead and do it.' I used to think green was a bad color, I used to avoid peanut shells, but not anymore. I've won doing things one way, and I've won doing things completely opposite. It comes down to hard work and preparation a lot more than it comes down to what little superstitions you have."

What has Gordon learned from his astonishing achievements as a race driver?

"God expects you to go out and do your job and do the best you can, but He doesn't want you to be controlled by that," he said succinctly.

ONLY A WEEK AFTER HIS FIRST TOP-FIVE FINISH OF THE 2000

SEASON, JEFF GORDON CHARGED BACK INTO VICTORY LANE, FOR THE

50TH TIME IN HIS YOUNG CAREER, AT NASCAR'S LONGEST AND

MOST PERILOUS TRACK, TALLADEGA SUPERSPEEDWAY, IN THE

DIEHARD 500.

QUITE SIMPLY, IT WAS SPECTACULAR.

WINSTON CUP | **youngest champion: 24 years of age**

24

Gordon started 36th in the 43-car field, only the eighth time in his career that he had failed to qualify for one of the 25 positions available in the first round. Since the 2.66-mile track was completed in 1969, no driver had ever won a race by coming from so far back.

"Great drivers are good fast, and good drivers are average fast. The fact that he's done so well in a relatively short time shows me a lot."

H.A. "Humpy" Wheeler, president of Lowe's Motor Speedway, in 1995

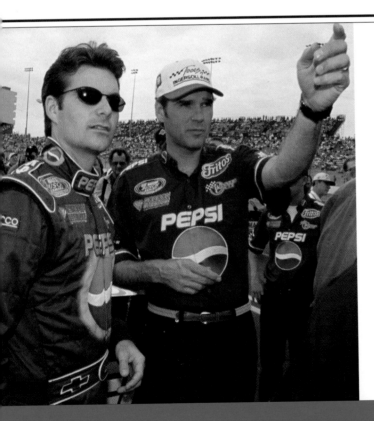

For 21 laps, Ford driver Mark Martin, twice a Talladega winner, held all his pursuers at bay. Then, with only five more laps to go, Gordon managed to draft past Martin in his familiar No. 24 Monte Carlo. From there, it was Gordon's turn to keep the pack of hounds, among whose number included teammates Mike Skinner and Dale Earnhardt, yapping safely behind him.

Skinner had never won an official Winston Cup race, and on the last lap he was hungry enough to block teammate Earnhardt, the most successful driver in the track's history. He was not, however, desperate enough to try to bump his way past Gordon and into victory lane.

Although he had the cooperation of Kenny Irwin, who drafted with him willingly until Skinner moved over to thwart Earnhardt, Skinner could not make a serious run on the ever-canny Gordon, who won at Talladega for the second time.

"The only way I was going to get by Gordon was if I ran in there real hard and just hit him," said Skinner, "and I wasn't going to do that. I didn't want to win the race that way. I think we've got a strong race team, and I think we can win without doing that to a guy [Gordon] who raced me as clean as he did all day."

Gordon's 50th victory overall was his 48th in a Monte Carlo
(his first two wins, in 1994, were in a Chevy Lumina),
meaning that he tied Darrell Waltrip for the all-time lead in
Monte Carlo victories. Earnhardt is third with 44.

"It's been an interesting year for us," said Gordon.
"I never lost faith in this team."

What Gordon also demonstrated was the fact that he was
still a contender for a fourth championship. The April 16 victory
bumped him from 12th to seventh in the point standings.

Dale Jarrett, who may have had the fastest car, had lost a lap when his Ford
ran out of gas. As long as his positioning could help his fellow Ford driver, Jarrett
did so. But once Gordon rose to the lead, and Martin found himself consigned
to sixth place, Jarrett obligingly moved over to let the four Chevrolets – Gordon,
Skinner, Earnhardt and Irwin – decide the race among themselves.

"Jarrett moved over like the gentleman that he is," said Gordon. "That helped out a lot because, when I was behind him, it was kind of messing me up."

A few days later, Gordon reflected on what his 50th victory – only seven drivers in NASCAR history had won more – meant.

"Talladega was a great confidence builder for the team," he said. "We wanted to get to victory lane, and we got there. You look at how competitive it is this year, and it's just unbelievable. Just to get to victory lane this year in the first nine races is pretty special for anybody. We're still looking for that consistency, and that doesn't mean we've necessarily got to go to every track and win. We want top fives and top 10s, and when we're in position at the end of races to win, we hope we can pull it off.

"I knew we were on the right track. I knew it was just a matter of time. But, for the people who aren't insiders, who don't know how good things have been going with our team, I think winning puts a lot of doubts to rest."

GORDON'S HUMILITY IMPRESSES HIS NEW CREW CHIEF

Late in 1999, brothers Rick and John Hendrick decided to look for a new crew chief for their team's leading driver, Jeff Gordon. The names of Gordon and Ray Evernham had become almost interchangeable, and Evernham had been more than just a crew chief for Gordon. He had been a mentor, a friend and a personal advisor.

But Evernham had decided it was time to move on. He had accepted a generous offer from DaimlerChrysler to manage Dodge's impending entry into the Winston Cup Series.

Brian Whitesell had been promoted late in 1999 to serve as crew chief in Evernham's absence, and Gordon had won the first two races, at Martinsville, Va., and Charlotte, with Whitesell calling the shots. But the team had then slumped in the final five races of the season.

What the Hendricks decided to do was elevate Whitesell to overall team manager, taking advantage of his immense administrative skills and hire Robbie Loomis as crew chief. Loomis brought to Hendrick Motorsports both considerable experience and personal qualities that Gordon would find appealing.

ON THE RELATIONSHIP BETWEEN JEFF GORDON AND RAY EVERNHAM:

"As an outsider, what you saw when you looked at this team, what you saw first was the success Ray and Jeff had in holding everything together," Loomis said, "and what you saw when you looked closely at that was that the relationship between Jeff and Ray had been much deeper than just driver and crew chief."

"Jeff's a very talented race-car driver," Loomis said, "but what Ray was really good at was picking out the things that Jeff didn't really talk about. He could see in Jeff's eyes and know when he wasn't quite happy with something. Even when Jeff would say things were OK, I think Ray could look at him and tell when things really weren't OK. He'd make the proper adjustments. That's probably the big thing Ray had going for him."

ON JEFF GORDON AS A PERSON:

"I just knew Jeff as a competitor," said Loomis. "Richard Petty told me he was one fine kid. 'One fine kid' is the way Richard said it, and Jeff really is. He has so many traits that remind me of the way Richard is, the way Richard handles certain situations. It amazes me, for a 28-year-old to have had the success he has had, the way he carries himself on the track and off the track.

"The one thing that amazed me the most was this. From the outside looking in, I thought he was too good to be true, that he was too squeaky-clean, but you know, he's like Richard [Petty]. What you see with him is what you get. He's so good that you just can't believe that a person behaves that way, handles bad situations the way he does. We've had our share of hardships early this season, and Jeff has done such a great job of keeping his cool. He told me, 'I've been through a lot rougher times than this,' and I've been through a lot rougher times than this, too."

ON THE CHARACTER OF JEFF GORDON:

"Richard always said, 'You can watch people when things are going well and you can't tell anything about them. You can watch them one minute when things are going bad and know everything about them.'

"Jeff's character just shines when he faces adversity. As much talent as he has, I think his greatest attribute is his humility."

ROBBIE LOOMIS

When Robbie Loomis became crew chief for Hendrick Motorsports' No. 24 team, he knew he had to develop a rapport with driver Jeff Gordon similar to Gordon's long-time relationship with Ray Evernham.

Loomis had worked with another NASCAR great, Richard Petty. Loomis, originally from Forest City, Florida, had been Petty's crew chief during "The King's" final two seasons as a driver, 1991-92. He then continued to work at Petty Enterprises for seven more seasons, as NASCAR's winningest driver adjusted to a new career as a team owner.

Rick Wilson, Jimmy Hensle, Wally Dallenbach Jr., Bobby Hamilton and John Andretti drove the famous Petty No. 43 during 1993-99.

During the 1999-2000 offseason, Loomis joined Hendrick Motorsports and became crew chief to the only driver ever to win three championships at a younger age than Petty.

RACE-DAY routine

ON A TYPICAL WINSTON CUP SUNDAY, HERE IS WHAT JEFF GORDON'S DAY WILL LOOK LIKE:

7:30 a.m. The race is five and a half hours away, and Gordon awakens in his motorcoach. It is parked in the infield. It is in an area equipped with utility hookups that is provided by the track. Gordon shaves, showers and enjoys a light breakfast, usually cereal.

8:15 a.m. "My routine works a lot around our sponsors," Gordon says. "These days, things are a little different, and I usually make an appearance or two for my sponsors on race morning." Typically, a golf cart or sport-utility vehicle transports Gordon to hospitality suites high above the track or large tents outside it. There he makes a brief appearance, says a few words and signs as many autographs as time will allow. In most cases, these promotional appearances are on behalf of DuPont Automotive Finishes, his primary Winston Cup sponsor, and Pepsi-Cola.

10 a.m. The race driver's grind is less regimented than his counterparts in other sports. He has no calisthenics, no batting practice, no lay-up lines. He has to attend the mandatory drivers' meeting, however, which is usually held in an area within the garage. Winston Cup officials discuss the individual characteristics of the track and race and preach caution, particularly to inexperienced drivers in the starting field. The format is not unlike that of the meeting at home plate before baseball games. Drivers and crew chiefs usually sit next to each other in the audience. The meeting usually concludes with a question-and-answer period.

10:30 a.m. Most drivers attend the worship service conducted by Motor Racing Outreach (MRO), and it is a vital part of Gordon's morning. The format is simple. Usually the service begins with a musical performance, followed by a sermon. Drivers sit with their families in the audience. The MRO service is also held in an area of the garage that has been cleared out for this purpose. It is not uncommon to find worshippers leaning against stacks of Goodyear racing tires.

11:15 a.m. Gordon walks to the team transporter, which has a lounge area in the front. "I come back and talk to Robbie [Loomis, the crew chief] and Brian [Whitesell, the team manager] a little bit. Then I stretch, because sometimes I do get cramps, up in the front of the transporter," Gordon says. "I've learned a few things down through the years. I stretch my lower back a little bit because that's what seems to hurt me the most the morning after a race. Then I get dressed, and I'll usually drink some kind of sports drink, something like a Gatorade."

11:45 a.m. Driver introductions are held on a platform of some sort, in front of the main grandstands. A few awards from the previous week are handed out, photos are taken, and the drivers walk across the stage and acknowledge cheers from the crowd.

12:15 p.m. Gordon gets in his race car, carefully straps himself in and puts on his helmet. "It's kind of like the same old routine, week after week after week," he says.

12:30 p.m. The race begins.

4 p.m. After the race, Gordon climbs from his car and is greeted almost immediately by media members. Usually the first to arrive are the radio and television commentators seeking live interviews. If he finishes second or third, he is accompanied to the infield media center for a brief press conference. If he wins, he goes to victory lane for the post-race celebration and photo ops, then takes part in an extensive post-race press conference, usually in the press box.

6 p.m. Gordon, accompanied by wife Brooke and a small entourage, is taken to a nearby airport and flies home via private jet.